Off Limits

Off Limits

Louise Wakeling

For my sons, Raj and Jesse

PUNCHER & WATTMANN

First published in 2021
Published by Puncher and Wattmann
PO Box 279
Waratah NSW 2298

http://www.puncherandwattmann.com
puncherandwattmann@bigpond.com

NATIONAL
LIBRARY
OF AUSTRALIA

A catalogue entry for this book is available from the National Library of Australia.

ISBN   9781922571021

Cover design by Miranda Douglas
Typesetting by Morgan Arnett
Printed by Lightning Source International

Australian Government

Australia
Council
for the Arts

This project has been assisted by the Australian Government through the Australia Council, its arts funding and advisory body.

Contents

Getting the picture

Futurama

Un-earthed

Earthed

Urbanites

Gunnamatta Bay, the Hacking River

float with the sticks on the stream – Virginia Woolf

loitering on a burnished deck, you know this place –
sea-grasses pollinating underwater, free-floating
Neptune's beads. dolphins scramble at the prow,
wavelets pluck the bows like a harp – somehow
you forget the renegade algae flagging you down
at the wharf, terrestrial inputs,
infilling sand smothering everything

wallowing in a slow surge from wharf to wharf
your mind strokes back through other summers,
those sticks swirling in the wake: spear-sharpening
grooves in Cabbage Tree Basin, Dharawal spirit-figures
and whales, canoes engraved on rocks, virgin forest
genuflecting in the wind, beaten-gold sunsets
and women's laughter on Jibbon Beach

the Curranulla's green and gold is throbbing
over shallow waters to Bundeena.
a gull peels away from the ferry
like blown paper, lifts and settles, origami
floating on meringue-tipped peaks. only then
the backlit city rises into view, questionable,
soundless, veiled in summer haze

The toad of White Bay

White Bay Hotel, squatted in, pissed on, landlocked:
you were always gonna burn, baby, burn —
(some idiot blogger puts his oar in:
if someone indeed torched this ugly toad
he did Sydney a huge favour)

only a matter of time before your bricks were levelled,
shovelled into the maws of bulldozers.
the enhancers of cities had their eye on you,
'visionaries' sized you up, calculated exactly
how valuable you were to them alive, how much

more so dead — such fine sweeping views across
the Anzac Bridge   that spider rolling over us
location location location
steamrolling over angles of vision
unimpeded now by your squat presence

white elephant, wharfies' watering-hole,
there one minute, gone the next — heritage
out the window   OUT IT GOES   gutted by fire,
a precinct waiting for developers to hey-presto —
smart eateries   million-dollar shoe-boxes —

high-rise heavens, window-boxes latching onto
grain silos like speed daters   disused rail yards
hooked up to a Master Plan: Anzac Bridge White Bay
Glebe Island, hub of a busy working port
plugged into the nation's meta-narratives of war
and heroism in muddy places
you were always
gonna burn baby burn

'Pred' and the Power Station

White Bay, Sydney

Where do I get a sense of timelessness? From huge dead machinery,
forgotten and abandoned…made of stuff forged in the fires of dying suns.
– Predator (deceased June 2004)

'Predator'   molecular biologist   caver
blogger *extraordinaire*   found poetry cut into a fence
in the Power Station at White Bay   acetylene-torched
into history. a drain-baby keen on coal-fired
sex in edgy places   'Pred' made love in corrugated
dark among rust broken glass and strange machinery

Stacey's watercolour *White Bay Power Station*
salutes Pred's posthumous blog-story – a hint of turrets
roof cascading red like blood down castle walls
deep frozen blood of the industrial revolution
a soft blur of tree   Harbour Bridge
muscling in on the horizon

I breathed deeply and regularly, 'Pred' wrote
and later I found I could not dream

locked down   barred and welded shut   but a cable port
could be wriggled through   sex in stale air freeing up
additional land capacity   exercising his rights:
'Public Access to Public Works'
his lover's breast and bum disappear
like Alice   tantalising in the gloom
their moment made edgier by torchlight
strafing dusty corners   Security
asking why he breaks into other people's
houses   anarcho-syndicalist   sometime squatter

good boy/bad boy   points out before strolling off
the Power Station isn't someone else's house

blogging three days before he died   death
doing its work on him   cells just following
instructions   says *it's coming for me.*
the sky is falling

moves into a deeper dark
all that strange machinery

Off limits

how they love to plumb the depths, stroke
the underbelly of a secret Sydney,
those headless *aficionados* of overflows
and undertows who surge like stormwater
through pipes, abseil down slippery slopes,
wriggle through eighteen-inch drains
you've got to admire the intestinal fortitude
of drain-waders because life above ground's
so...well, drained, so topside − not like
those strange stalactites, iron-red
and hanging from the roof, white mushroom
clouds of fungus, Moreton Bays dangling
roots like dark webs overhead, cold surge
of ocean at the Fortress's gaping mouth,
moon and street-lights so beautiful at Lurline Bay −

only the chosen go to ground in tunnels
fumigated for their convenience − for all
they know, crocodiles of the Nile play
the strumpet there; snapping turtles
grow fat on frogs and rats, meet up
with Ninja pals or plot a heist, *Rififi*
themselves into the flooded basements
of merchant bankers in Macquarie Street,
infiltrate defence force installations
or suburban flats storeys up in Coogee Bay

they never know who they're going to meet
down there − IT boys and office workers,
students slaving for degrees in Recreational
Trespass, Cave Clanners and girl graffiti-
artists on fold-up scooters bent on going

where they're not supposed to:
theirs is a kind of moratorium
on compliance: in the absence
of Vietnams and tsunamis, they satisfy
an urge for diving into the wreckage,
sewer-surfing the past, thumbing their noses
at all those 'thou shalt nots' a city's
predicated on, the obverse of our 'clean
and green', dedicated drain-spotters
seeking poetry in other people's motions

Harbourings

seahorses cling to trolleys at the bottom of the Harbour
stayin' alive under wharves   among eel-grass and algae beds
the Authorities confer: what to do about fishing
in Port Jackson — meetings scheduled in offices are deep enough
in sludge to bury three men standing on each other's shoulders

fishermen still trawl surfaces with lines   gloating over rows
of silvery flesh — but the word is 'catch and release'   a mantra
for the times   unless you fancy Toxic Shock at sunset
on the Beulah Street Wharf at Kirribilli   a creeping
accumulation in the blood

white-bellied sea-eagles   oblivious   print-challenged   feed
their chicks dioxin cocktails from Homebush Bay   winging
and wheeling from open river mouth to the yellow foam
of heavy-metal bays   soaring above playing fields into a livid sky
that old refinery flare with burning gas   then floating carcasses,
bedraggled slump of feathers on nests in Newington

upstream near the Lennox Bridge at Parramatta it's the Carp Fish Out
a Vietnamese fisherman plucking silver from the river
a gentle tug   they rise   flat and sleek   to gobble air   whiskers
twitching like a cat's   (they don't need much oxygen to thrive
roiling and blowing out mud and plants from the river bottom)

at Silverwater   the wash of a Rivercat surges and hisses
against the mangroves   a young boy saunters past a skull
and crossbones   jauntily shouldering his catch

Archaeological dig, Town Hall

we wait for friends before the march, sprawled
on a curve of marble steps, like this city waits,
on heat for the tight pods of agapanthus
to burst onto the scene, jacaranda
to explode in purple

under the clock tower, under the grinning lions,
archaeologists record, measure, photograph.
time washes over the graves like aquatints,
geological strata, souls trapped
like fossil-fish in sediment

graves are unearthed from time to time,
skulls gape at sudden daylight. tiles
on the mansard roof ripple like an inland sea,
lap at their own reflections
in the mirror-balls of cinema complexes

in the Peace Hall men straddle coffins,
grasp clipboards among a jumble of dust
and wood, shards of bone,
these dark spaces beneath our lives, lozenges
of darkness angled beneath east and west,

here where the unnamed mother lay,
infant nearby, breath scarcely drawn.
convict and free are jumbled together
seam after seam over the yes-place
of the Gadigal, those onlookers

in Hyde Park, fringe-dwellers in cast-off clothes
faintly sketched in watercolours of the early colonists,
to one side of the canvas, as though
they were ghosts already

it's business as usual for the living. city fathers plan
their thrusting infrastructure smack-bang
in the middle of the commercial district,
a Second Empire 'wedding-cake' to erase
the relics of the past. carriages roll
under the *porte-cochère*, pale girls
in *tableaux vivants* channel Sarah Bernhardt
under the chandeliers

graves are exhumed, bones re-located
to the Devonshire cemetery,
the 'wedding-cake' rises in tiers
as the town bloats, toad mimicking an ox,
Napoleonic grandeur grafted onto bones

the disused cemetery flaunts its effluvia
beyond the wall, unsavoury characters urinate
on tombstones, thieves bury stolen goods
among headstones, and larrikins deface
what they cannot fathom

Gadigal middens are buried
under Angel Place, though women
still fish in canoes at Warrane, gather
cockles from sandy beaches. smoke rises
from gunyahs in the Domain.

secretly, at night, a father brings his still-born baby,
folds her gently in the earth. over the wall, the clip-clop
of carriage-horses in George Street,
howls of barking dogs.
a late-night fiddle scrapes at air

before the broad arrow the black
and yellow of repeat offenders
before Macquarie saw the place
as a series of aesthetic landscapes
before freshwater streams became sewers

before the wall Macquarie built
to keep the hordes out of the Domain
(climbed over, holed,
circumvented somehow)
before suicides were buried
in Hyde Park with stakes through their hearts
and men were carted to the hanging grounds
at Brickfield Hill   before smallpox
brought its eerie silence to the coves
and riverbanks of Warrane...

swamp lilies grew along the shore
white spider-flowers rose from wet soil
stamen and anthers bruised-purple
the colour of congealed blood
bronze-wing pigeons flew spear-straight
metallic patches catching light
men dived for shellfish in the shallow waters,
shadowy girls tossed whelks
and mud-oysters to waiting friends,
a ringed moon over the bay

In the 'hood
Ermington

in this Sleepy Hollow, neighbours don't talk
to neighbours; there's no shared language
for suburban inwardness. the cars of perfect strangers
ping-pong out of driveways, slot back in again
with cuckoo-clock precision.

houses are a *Fallingwater* of winter detachment,
angular, no curves of light in this frozen wood,
only Hokusai prongs of ice and arrested movement.
these houses are not on the *Smithsonian's* Life List
of 28 places "to visit before you die".

disembodied laughter and the sounds
of children playing indoors. a piano warms up
like a cat mincing on keys. the street prickles
with the shrieks of birds, the 24/7 yapping
of a penned-up lapdog, nose snuffing
at the outside world with fury.
he'll never let up telling them good fences
make dogs that keep on keeping on.

sometimes, before rain, you're watching clouds
dark-faced and sombre, and the dull whine
of a lawnmower frets and chops at the air.
the sky flings the first drops of rain at windows,
big and splashy, and trees defer to rising wind

at dusk there's the swish of rain on trees,
the soft wet drag of tyres on the road; night flows
slick as a black river past liquid-ambars.
memories rise like the cries of plovers at dusk

Urban sprawl

a bush-rat springs along the fence at sunset,
dog angst and territorial obsession frisson in the dusk
the intruder skittering across low-slung branches
of the Moreton Bay like a blurred memory
on feral nights bats do circus tricks upside down
on ripening fruit   the tree hogs its cramped space
bird-seeded   unplanned   far from any park
a tight foothold for squirrel gliders   a high-rise of possum
owl blinking on and off like a men-at-work sign
frogs opt for silence   something beaked
and vigilant waits in darkness

purslane semaphores from cracks in the footpath
outside Vinnies   spread-eagled   trodden flat
medicinal properties unreleased from tear-drop leaves
Garden Nazis hate it but recipes proliferate on blogs
like spy-bots over enemy terrain   everyone's a Columbus
discovering purslane on the verge of parks   edged out
by council workers   zapped by pesticides   grubbed out
by developers   now suddenly fashionable   a known unknown
like organic egg farmers and farm-gate hopefuls
in the outer 'burbs   this food-bowl of the endless city

off Windsor Road another something   sky-hooked predator
vixen maybe   tears apart Trav's chickens   hell-bent
on survival   dug-out swarming with new arrivals   or a dog fox
flashing across a six-lane highway   grinning   bearing his brush
like a flag   next morning   the only evidence
a smear of blood and feathers on grass   there are suburbs
out here where you can drive around and around
and never get your bearings   one gable or porch like another
as panic sets in   surfaces don't absorb and street signs

point at the sky   but that other life goes on, insistent
oblivious to encroaching townhouses
developers red in tooth and claw
and all our dead-end behaviour
in the bitumen foothills of our town

Drive-by moments

Spurway Street, 11 a.m., day after New Year, a drive-by shooter
sprays an empty car with bullets. opposite, Christmas reindeer
haul sleighs of sparkling lights across the turf, surfing Santas hang ten
on roofs, strangled Santas dangle from gutters like failed housebreakers.
crime-scene tape festoons the road, the new tinsel.

once the population centre of Sydney,
statistically speaking. a pie chart
divvies us up: workers, homeowners, mortgagees,
a few unemployed. the new aspirationals.

that's one of them sitting cross-legged
on the pavement outside "For the Love of Sausages":
hey babe − you wouldn't have
a coupla dollars you could lend me?

in the Housing Commission flats on Bartlett St.
a grey doona rots on a balcony, year in, year out,
sprouts mildew, spills stuffing like ruptured grey matter.
rooms re-assemble on the kerb, empty drawers
recline like odalisques at crazed angles,

bristling with the surreal clarity of a Magritte.
The Difficult Crossing, maybe, a severed hand
clasping a pigeon, a baluster eyeballing unhinged windows.
next door, some wag has amended
the street numbering to 'nits 31-50'.

down on the waterfront, a vandalised George Kendall Reserve
courts new neighbours in the Riverwalk Estate,
prime land carved to the bone: noses in the air,
million-dollar townhouses hump the levee

above the toxic naval dump. a desolate path
along the river affronts apartments in the latest style
only the rich and vacant can afford.

the sign in the Reserve gives *Dietary Advice*:
these words are the new black, the shade of bland
that councillors and bureaucrats aspire to.
gone are the official skull and crossbones,
fish struck out with a crimson bar.
casual fishermen are reminded only
that unsafe levels of dioxins *might* make their catch unpalatable

Long-distance affair

MGM Grand, Vegas

Here, sex means sex. – Donald Revell

lovers navigate this endless Ark   shy now in mirrored lifts
where recent sex still clings like honeydew to skin
(but a downcast woman in the lift   back to the wall
has blown it all at baccarat)

we wander corridors like stretch-limos carpeted
in tunnel-vision red (*everything is here* in this transient city)
amazed   a thousand Ariadnes unravel through mirrored
multiplying exits   pursuing Theseus or the Minotaur
(that's you hanging the 'Recharging' sign on the door)

we switch off the light   reinvent ourselves the way the city does
re-combine like neon atoms or mist rising from the Bellagio Fountain –
feral women   demon lovers reaching into each other
for something like redemption

outside, you look down at a blank wall
flat   featureless   shutters that don't open
but Mexican voices   somewhere   warm as enchiladas

Road-trip, New Mexico

1.
stand in a juniper forest you say
juniper is succour   protection
its bark exfoliates in strips
seeds follow the call of gravity   dispersed
by birds and wind   mammalian purgings
so many slow-germinating seeds
falling on dry ground

stand in a juniper forest you say
I savour the silence of leaves
crushed between fingers:
when aromatic juniper occupies
the higher ground   evil scatters

stand in a juniper forest you say
but already they're sparser here
on the road out of New Mexico
dwindling fast as they lose elevation −
where does forest end and desert begin?

common mountain junipers   twisted and sculpted
cede to sagebrush and Saguaro   some farmers
burn them   chop them down
water-hungry thieves of cattle they say

2.

finding someone else's footsteps on the trail
you track them   swallowed up by junipers
I give up trying to work you out
the road's gone   I'll never find the car
though it's there   like the gun
in the glovebox   on the side of the road
dusty and glinting
in another dimension

sinking in red sand – wrong shoes   wrong mood
for this high-noon heat – I breathe the smoke
of a silence that spooks me   step on
the shadow of the gunman that haunts
this country   do I want to be here alone
beside the road   imagining?

Memento mori at Little Beach, Maui

we climb the bluff with two mermaids you've latched onto
gregarious as ever   drumming up a faded dream of youth
a sunset playing with fire   naked bodies thrumming
to the beat of waves   scramble through a cleft of lava rock
on knives to Little Beach   the track pitches and falls
rough-going at first — we scrabble like crabs and slide
down yielding sand on a heave of hill   shadows like caves
unlock this not-so-well-kept-secret sacred place
African talking drums are garrulous as seagulls
a tide of turquoise water pooling at our feet.
who could tire of burnished flesh and bongos at dusk,
resist the twirling hoops of fire? you're not quite
up for such depravity, but you'd love to bum
a Mary-Jane from dreadlocked dudes, or maybe
Aphrodite there, passing between sand and sea
like a golden flame — even without glasses, you've seen
how beautifully her body defies the pull of gravity

Siege mentality

your words a Great Wall of stones
built against intrusions or incursions,
Earth Dragon of brick and masonry.
but the fortress has fallen
here and there among long grass

I can't have that conversation again,
you say. my words are femurs
poking from ramparts, eye sockets
in the skulls of long-dead defenders.
they lie among the bones of invaders
who leapt those barriers –
moss grows on bones and tumbled stones alike

for two years our words have streaked
across oceans – comets, remnants, glowing
lumps of ice, diminishing, rushing
against time. I knew what comets meant,
from the beginning. syllables now
hollow as blown eggshells in dry grass.

distance swallows gestures, language
a hard-won kiss pulled from you
in an unguarded moment.
your fortifications stretch for miles
in all directions, bristling with armaments.

you'll wait it out,
for death or your dream life – solitude
and a warm ocean, sailboat tacking
into the wind, another passion to erase
the last. my words disappear
like dwindling rain over parapets

Take-off

you were smiling with the usual emoticon –
cheesy grin, black glasses signalling
'nudge nudge, wink wink' – not iconic at all
because later you backed off faster
than a speeding Alaskan Airways jet
hoisting you up up and away   air-pockets
above volcanoes   to your manifest destiny

later   skype was not an option
you couldn't manage your face anymore
too much back-tracking in it
eyes skeetering into the middle distance

in the cabin your head touched the ceiling
leaving Maui at thirty-five thousand feet
and those remnants you recalled –
three frangipani blossoms on a ledge
should have told me   not to mention
the exploding sink emptying
at the touch of a button and your view
that one Paradise after another
is not up to scratch I wasn't
anywhere in that scenario

the indifferent beaches of Maui
crawl with tourists swimming like insects
against the tide you said (of course *you*
weren't one of them)   you'd get island fever
if you stayed there
even with the dream sailboat
a warm ocean   the numbing drumming
and a feral bunny to give you
your morning dose

yes   turbulence gets around
you said   on a plane bound somewhere else

We might all be cactus

at your other house in Arizona you could walk out
drunk and fall into the arms of a Mexican Ocatillo.
spiky limbs dissect the pathway to the door, and I
get the feeling I'll never make it out alive.

everyone knows what a cactus is —
the stuff of obsession. spines pierce flesh and spirit
if you're not careful. some give them a wide berth.
handle them gingerly? you better.
they're prickly and quirky as a room full of poets.
they stick around. they're in for the long haul,
and you're not in it. who would collect them?
sadists or lovers? are they prickly horror,
or plant with personality? that "so Dr. Seuss"
cat-in-a-hat-creative shock of green-eggs-and-ham,
porcupine spines and a riot of colour,
mandala flowers that persuade you (for a moment)
there might be something in that dumb theory
of intelligent design — but no, cacti perfect
as blown-glass paperweights, fine-tuned
to the universe, so elegantly evolved.
at least they don't indulge in puddle thinking,
smugly sure the universe is fortunate
to have them in it. survivors?
we could all take a leaf out of their book

Some like it hot

is this one 'Death', and that for wusses only, voyeurs who like
to watch what must be hot stuff going down some other gullet,
not their own? or are these chillies for *aficionados* who dare

each other to down a brown *Moruga* whole — two of them —
like "Ted the Fire-breathing Idiot", who takes the youtube challenge
to slowly masticate two pods of the *Trinidad Scorpion Butch T*

guaranteed to leave him writhing for the next few hours. if only
he was a seagull, with non-existent heat receptors, chomping a Habanero
in the Taco wagon car-park — no harm done, you say. true chilli lovers know

the pain is fake, the heat a blind, an evolutionary trick to throw
marauding mammals off the scent. this pumped-up "holy water"
turns men and even feisty tattooed girls into gibbering idiots,

high on endorphins, orgasmic, and aching for cold milk.
it's only the intention to hurt that causes pain,
however uber-real that red hot poker down your throat.

in chillies as in love: "go hard", the growers say, "or stick to ketchup"

The gift

that bottle of Carolina Reaper
sauce sitting in my pantry —
sent halfway round the world
it mouths your last challenge.
a death's head grins at me
every time I open the door.
a parting gift,
or a chilli grenade
lobbed into my kitchen?

I win hands down, half a teaspoon
in a bowl of guacamole
to your single drop in a vat
of chilli con carne.
I guess I can handle the heat.
small consolation —
you reaped, ploughed
me back in. it was always
a competition, wasn't it?

Answer to *The Couple's Tao Te Ching*

you can't hug a Saguaro — we both know that. I've tried it,
in a spirit of craziness or satire or because some of us, we're innate
tree-huggers, and Saguaro seem so — personable. yes, I know,
this flowing love binds you and your beloved to all things in creation
they stand there in the desert, waving and pointing and semaphoring,
wanting a conversation, giving us the thumbs up, or sometimes
the rude finger. forget that spirit of the West stuff — as though the Saguaro
has *anything* to say about Manifest Destiny or Westward ho! the wagons

still, they tempt us. we read faces, arms and limbs akimbo, see cowboys
in dusty high-noon streets. survivalists, really, bunkered down in the desert,
weapons at the ready like a border vigilante. a threatened species.
every part of them, gesture and language, beautiful and useful:
a hollow for birds, so Tao, extravagant, night-blooming, nectar flowing
to long-nosed bats in the flowering season

let's face it — they're damn prickly, and we can only mimic intimacy,
mock-hug something that lets us know it means business if we try
to get too close. keep a respectful distance from those spines, girl —
like lovers who say *you just want more than I can give* —
they're armed to the teeth, and will protect themselves

Migrations and transplantations

Joe's story, 1961

'the *kafeneion* is like – icon – us Greeks
bin everywhere, Katoomba, Ipswich, Gundagai,
we have Paragon, Elite, Ellisos...
here – work – she *never* finish.
my wife, she make chips all day, peel potatoes –
cook hamburgers, sausage and egg –
no way Greek food – you crazy?
my customers, they take me outside,
they shoot me, run me out of the town –
ohi, sometime we take to neighbours
real food, my wife make *galaktoboureko*,
dolmades, *moussaka*, they like –
but in Australia, *kafeneion* is spaghetti
on toast, boiled haddock, talk, drink coffee...
Maria even she cook hot day, sick, rain –
never stop, vegetable garden, lemon tree.
she get baby – never stop. we come here,
start new life for our children – *ne*, Toula,
Georgina, little Maria – they very smart,
talk English very good – yes, *efharisto*,
I learn some English in the shop – very poor
but everyday talking, farmers, miners –
sometime drunk, Friday night they call me
'bloody dago', they say 'we no eat in your shop
no more' and now Maria she want go back,
but I say no, always they come, eat my food,
American food, sundaes, Soda Fountain,
limonade Spider, Australian food – mixed grill,
fried pork chop – is good life here, *good* people.
we fight together in Greece, we Greeks
and you Australians, *andaxi*, ok
we not forget the Germans' occupation...

I was in the mountains with the *andartes*,
guerillas – after the war, Greeks killing Greeks –
politics, pah, I spit on that! – but all past,
I tell Maria, this is new country,
this is the beginning,
we make Hellas *here*'

Two Studies for Maria

1.

shipwrecked

leaning into the wind, she faces down
the afternoon glare, the burning edge of things,
wants to be anywhere but here,
shipwrecked on the veranda of a café.
the life of this town is the colour of the dust
on Main Street, flat, one-dimensional.
her feet grip the boards like olive trees
along the coast road to Xampelia.

herbs in pots barely sustain her, dry as the track
beyond the town; folded arms
ward off the evil eye. the aging mother
Adamantia broods, a world away in Mytilene,
the father lingers at the *ouzeri*,
and *her* the guilty one for leaving home —
the groaning ship plunging and rearing
through dark seas to the mainland

2.

the return

flat-footed, beyond weary the apron tells you,
she takes a moment's respite, hands tinctured
with garlic and thyme, potatoes sliced

on the board , her perfect *galactoboureko*
drowning in orange-flavoured syrup
on the kitchen table.

this afternoon, for her friends
Athena and Lavrentis, she will unpack
the special coffee she has brought from Greece.

there will be laughter on roof-tops,
hillsides starred with wildflowers,
neighbours calling to her from the *kafeneio*.

*goats pick their way past Turkish minarets
on ancient dizzying cliffs.   clouds are hovering gulls
above a blue-green sea.   she is crossing Kremasti Bridge again,
stone by stone.*

Backs to the wall

blind seers decree fences stretching into oceans
waders might cross to promised lands
gated communities keep the poor out
'invading hordes' dammed   stemmed
blocked   because it's unimaginable
we should have bridges   commingling
and still they keep coming like the tides
of our own ancestors   spilling
across the borders of others
moving in darkness

the builders of walls pile brick on brick
steel ramparts rising against imagined foes
walls to keep people out   walls
to keep people in   scaled
or torn down − people have danced
on the rubble of walls   souvenired
masonry − fast-forward
flags flutter above coiled razor wire
new ogres growling "you shall not pass"
and no   the Great Wall of China
cannot be seen from the moon
with the naked eye

Epitaph for a Sydney drug-runner

Andrew Chan was executed by firing-squad in Indonesia, 2015

redemption, of a kind, was what he was after, breath,
but the death he perfected was
all that he won,
the poetry of dying, a grace-note, how it was done.
a powerful Church stage-managed the hearse.
an octet of prisoners singing themselves to death,
while in the Hills, advertising hype weds chapter and verse.

Passing trade

she's one of Robert Pinsky's *jaunty, crop-haired greying*
women   the kind you see in supermarkets   and yes her hips
aren't bad   but she stares back with a look that shows her
planted in the world   defiant   a rock in her own home

B&B guests come and go   slide into her life sideways
admire the quirky paintings   girl leaping a tiger
in a blur of orange   her Guatemalan armadillo
and goggle-eyed frog fraternising on a shelf

some show their scars, real or otherwise — the finger
sanded to the bone, one suicide on the job too many
(she has a listening face) — how life has torn at them
left them halting   unsure of their reception

fifteen years in tunnels and on tracks   orange vest
high-viz in her sunroom   bald patch   grey frizz
at the centre like a monk's tonsure   he rough-trades
the sounds of suffering for her seafood chowder

self-confessed loner   abandoned by teenage parents
a fall backwards on a building site three floors down
onto concrete — brain not right   he peers
through glass wondering aloud if those hydrangeas
in a green milk-jug are real   "I really like your house",
he says   she hears his real or spiel   she's not sure which
more grounded anyway than the call-centre voice
purporting to be from "Rear Windows" wanting
to pry into her computer

he moves on to the failed marriage   the Samoan
heritage   the flakiness of former partners   soup cold
now in the bowl   she's on the same page   naturally inclined
to observe others but wary after the *Sturm und Drang*

of her own couplings   "How old *are* you?" he asks
for the fifth time   even when he makes a semi-pass
retracted soon as made (in her kitchen now rinsing bowls)
the gust of his need is not "unlovable" she thinks
third eye focussing like high-powered binoculars
a current of warm air connecting them   blowing
across the chill spaces of the room

You should leave the country like Gogol

for Robert McNicol

go Roman before summer's red-hot poker
sears the skin like roasted eggplant and the place
becomes impossible – that little seaside town

in Norway beckons like an old man putting his feet up
by the water, maybe the Old Man of the Dovrë himself
and you won't even notice the iced-over mountain

squatting there like a troll-courtier in the great Hall
(you'll be too busy hiding from the troll-witches
wielding knives, ice in the blood)

but now the driveway cops the flak
of jacaranda flowers, their hitchhiker bees
tumbling in fluted heaven

already Mauvember's launched its spring offensive
and you can't leave now, with that tree rolling out
its welcome mat, upturning your heart, rolled

over like a stone and warming on the other side.
a captured asteroid, you're stuck in earth's orbit,
your interplanetary probe won't lift you
up to Mars.   here's the prospect:
vertigo, forever falling from mountains
into the fading soundtrack of the world,

or going forward on all fours,
the world spinning on its crazed axis,
restlessness prickling like heat rash.

you're not hungry for Tahitian pearls
in Beijing Friendship stores or fitting room Nirvanas
in Hong Kong, just on-again off-again road affairs

memorable as skunk-stripes tattooed on US Interstate 82
the heart in a trajectory at last, am-tracking
its own fault-lines and desert places   plotting

fresh horizons, the way stoop labour might dream:
asparagus-cutters, bent double at the waist,
slashing at green spears in a dusty field

Getting the picture

'Sandmining, Main beach, 1956'

It was the raping of our foreshore – Margaret Olley

a memory of green suffuses this landscape
tincture of cane-fields   rainforest and mountains
of Tully   she remembers banksias
and cottages   assertive grasses compete
for line honours with pipes and shadows

in Olley's painting seagulls hover
above a cone spewing minerals
the worker squinting at coils
but there's balance here
bold lines in charcoal and pencil
a quiet interrogation of structure
green splashes on spinifex
squat, intrusive   the extractor
sucks out black sand heavy
with rutile and ilmenite
foreshores implode   middens fractured
sand turns to slime   profits funnelled
to America   titanium deployed
for space-craft and guided missiles
strong   unreactive   unlike beaches

White, Whitely, Whitest

after Brett Whitely, *Portrait of Patrick White at Centennial Park, 1979-80*

a face left wondering whether truth can be the greatest destroyer of all
– Patrick White, *Flaws in the Glass*

White, salient one, baleful stare of a newly-minted Zombie, loose-armed
and boneless in his chair, likes dogs without collars, hates the overgrown
school prefects we're lumbered with in public life: *verboten* lists of likes
and hates legible to all: even today, we tie ourselves in knots to read them
in the gallery (though who could argue with that, watching
the latest politicians twist and turn in the wind?)

the whole thing a collage of Brett himself, nothing literally true, "The House",
bone-white claws   scratched us awake, teeth of the Great White bit us
into consciousness, artist and icon introducing a new continent to itself.
and no sprinkler in the front garden, no bird-feeder, the wrong aspect
from Centennial Park, where they walked – young man, old man,
companionable, the view east, not north – even Manoly, calm and kindly –

a satyr-faced Significant Other leering from a frame, owlish,
vaudeville, like one of the Marx brothers…what's that about?
and a sprawling erotic magnolia – a cluster of pistils clutched by stamens,
image lifted from another work, androgynous, Brett the wild young artist

drunk on White's chaise longue after boozy dinners, taken up, at first, a delight,
an odalisque – idolised, tolerated, dropped. the charge: dishonesty, betrayal.
White, furious. never liked being snagged on another man's 'truth'.
the artist deleted the exchange.   like it never happened.

Out of harm's way (*Lavender's blue*)
after Brett Whitely, *Art, Life and the other Thing, 1978*

a hand offers a syringe, Lavender Bay
turned Lavender's blue, far beyond blue,
a silent roar, simian creature handcuffed
and nailed through the arms like a bizarre Christ.
baboon rages, bared fangs in the garden
of earthly delights, paradise well and truly lost

the craving fuels art, it seems, like crawling
into blown eggs with other displaced persons,
being prodded into cauldrons by apes
with pitchforks (Bosch has a lot to answer
for when distortion's its own god)

no excuse except the pursuit of Art
with a capital A by the rebel
bringing home the bacon — and home it came
with New York exhausted (Art
can't change anything, he found)
Fiji a no-go zone for busted opium-eaters

nowhere else was it *that* blue, ultramarine,
like the harbour cut by the wake of a boat
or the flight of a white bird. wild Fijian hair,
signature frangipani brooch his good luck charm,
opulent nudes — all that *optical ecstasy,*

at least until morphine welded
to receptors in the brain turns
pleasure to pain, invention to ashes

Totem 1 (Brett Whitely)

what to make of it, the get laid totem,
fibre glass egg in a black nest?
a good lay, if nothing else, sex
in the city − bright egg on a black nest,
black totem colonised by whiteness,
swollen with borrowed meanings,
contraries he revelled in,
fascination with the dark impending other

or is it a balancing act, icon fertilised
by layers of other meanings,
a Selenite egg for the ancient goddess
of the moon? will it dispel confusion,
ensure we see the bigger picture?

in the artist's peripheral vision,
an end-stopped life kept coming, coiled
in Bosch-inspired eggs cracked open
and spilling tortured men and women,
headless trunks and torsos half-ingested
by demons − Christie in Ladbroke Grove
with his mutilated women,
totem's serrated teeth

Cheekily conflating a painting or two

for Reg Mombasa

They turned everything upside down...they turned everything
inside out... – from "Those who see the other side", Dog Trumpet

Taronga roars its approval across the water at these curled clippings
on the foreshore, sunset-stained, clippers inspired by the wind,
anchored on Bennelong's birthplace, moored now in our DNA.
the wings of this house fly away from a Waikiki of building blocks,
Lego legacy of matchbox towers and toasters that pass for architecture
in this new millennium

sure, we weren't quite ready for Mombasa effrontery,
like the Beer Monster at the Sydney Olympics, vetoed for his penis-tap
frothing beer, or Australian Jesus dispensing gifts for refugees
in unjust Australia. (here, location comes before equity, sport
before subsidies for the arts: think drunken footballers crapping
in hotel corridors, overpaid clowns groping pussy in city bars)

but the Op House has taken root, reinvented on a billion tea-towels,
white notes dropped into blue. snow-dome blizzards bizarrely
powder noses, a cockatoo raises its perky crest on Dame Edna's
outlandish *Ascot Ladies' Day Hat, 1976*, the heavy machinery
of Opera House Glasses, so in-your-face, up yours with diamantes,
giraffes crane necks above trees, startled by the vision of something different:
snow and ice tiles melt in rainbow hues, sailboats tacking backwards
and forwards, crescent moons waxing and waning on dark water

Looking west

after Jeff Rigby's *Looking West from the Roof, 204 Clarence Street, 1986*

above Clarence street, knife-edge
buildings tempt the suicide in us all.
brutal planes of high-rise mock
a flattened Pyrmont, sandstone cliffs
long quarried out, fading images
of Pirrama's bubbling spring

smoke-stacks of Pyrmont B
abut the river, heavy industry's
four-fingered salute to a hard-bitten
CBD where Silver and the Lone Ranger
gallop endlessly on surfaces
against a sky rinsed pale in winter light

Pyrmont's AC/DC fuelled the city's hunger
for power, Star Casino rising
from its ashes — "Sydney's Viagra",
crowed its CEO. high rollers
getting higher on *sic-bo*
and chuck-a-luck and Grand Hazard

for me the city flows two ways, still,
alternating past and future — the bones
of offices long gone imprint their auras,
windows archive the shapes of buildings,
a ghost tour of rooftops and bridges
sliding into the slipstream of a winter's day

Wolf-peaches

after Nora Heysen's *Tomatoes, 1939*

"plump thing with a navel",
Cortés discovered you growing
in Montezuma's gardens,
brought your seeds back to Europe —
a showy curiosity
designated not for eating

tomatoes ripen in a bowl, the colour
of becoming. your contours resile
from certainty — are you *pommes d'amour,*
fruit or vegetable, poisonous or not?
state fruit/state vegetable,
Arkansas has you both ways

pale, blue patterned, the bowl
enfolds you, knowing
you're grounded, the way you bowed
to the earth with your own weight,
sprawled without support,
riotous on the vine. I'd stake

my life on you, seeding all over
the place, between bricks,
at a side gate, promiscuous
among daisies, no respecter
of borders, time-traveller
on the beaks of birds

one day, hot tomatoes, red — ripe for it —
plucked from a garden somewhere,
you bring the outside inside.
I'll wait until you're good
and ready, and then I'll have you,
right there on the kitchen table

this poem doesn't give a damn
about cantaloupes,
only the way a shaft of sunlight
transforms you, a warm room
brings you on, wolf-peaches
in a curve of china

Happy hour
after Helen Grove's *Doing Happy Hour, 2010*

you're smiling in that pink space, magpie
and cat book-ending your day,
outsized cuppa — you've got it all
in hand, angst-free time on the couch
down-time from grave thoughts
arrowing in through morning's
slatted blinds. cat's rolling free
at your feet, leg askew
like a stray thought, or sadness banished.
happiness is not an obligatory work-out
or the false glow of positive thinking —
it's the full frontal of your steady gaze,
afternoon rituals, letting sleeping dogs lie,
magpie eye-balling morsels
on the verandah, libations of tea

At the Mosman Art Gallery

I can only look at a pooch in a bathtub so many times,
says the art collector to his 'friend with benefits'
the more abstract the better, elephant-trunk splashes,
swathes of red and green, something from Guadalupe,
not this quirky Aussie realism, Lucy Culliton's
washed-out Deco green and yellow from a bygone era

ah, she says, establishing difference, I love
the mundaneness of it — toilet, shell-shocked dog —
banal, like clothes-racks in the Good Room.
we feel his pain, bath-bound, one-eyed, freedom beyond.
the painter wills the dog to stay, he's sheepish,
but patient with her standing orders,
fills up the emptiness with his anxious face.

"I see fight-or-flight", she says, "still-life itching
to escape the label: 'Nude in Bathtub (wet or dry)' —
she wants to paint her bathroom with someone in it."
salience. a purpose. over on the bedroom wall
the tattooed bruiser's cavorting in his Santa hat.
bathrooms have such complex resonances —
not just for mutts, she murmurs, moving on

Futurama

'We live in exponential times'*

we haven't had an upgrade
in more than a thousand years
Peter Diamandis reminds us
evolution is mandatory –
robotics   AI networks   sensors
accessible to everyone = Enhanced Empathy
+ the wisdom of Solomon

we'll care more about elephants
killed for their tusks and chemical streams
glowing in a grey dawn

what's the alternative   become house-pets
playthings of AI   algae clinging to a dead planet?
better to connect our finite brains to clouds
that rain down infinite information
keep companies exponentially
seeding into the future   mining metals
on far-off asteroids   fossicking in space
eager for first contact with trillion-dollar deals

no mysteries to fathom   knots to undo
no hosannas   no grief   no point
clinging to it   I guess   mere humanity
earth will let us go   puffed
into the stuff of asteroids

---

* Professor Zachary Dodds, Computer Science Department, Harvey Mudd College, CA
Peter Diamandis, Engineer and entrepreneur, founder of the X Prize Foundation

but out there   in some distant galaxy
watching ten moons rise over iron-rich mountains
we'll look like humans from a distance
merged with machines and maximising consumption.
we'll be God-like, Professor Dodds predicts
funnier   sexier   we'll remember everything

Flirting with the future

give me back my broken night,
my mirrored room, my secret life.
It's lonely here.
– Leonard Cohen

assuming we'll still exist we'll die older with bigger brains and stem-celled
new eyes still peering into crystal balls at star burn-outs and hit-or-miss
asteroids though we've barely understood the past

nothing about certifiables in the White House and climate refugees
going under swelling oceans   all border forces erased
despite the best walls money can buy

there'll be no fish   of course   or they'll be skinnier
global wildfires will have burnt us back to the essentials
of a charred earth

it's all good – we'll be strutting the catwalks on a terra-formed Mars
in our Solar nanotech wearable technology only the rich can afford
mutated beyond recognition but still arguably human

our fossilised cities will be known to archaeologists only
by their buried tunnels and utilities   Detroit-is of a stalled planet

we can always leave an avatar to think for us in perpetuity
upload our digitalized consciousness to a cloud somewhere
spilling our emptiness into an infinite flat universe
good to know

The Spirit of *Curiosity*

quite a road trip, that first landing
Spirit bouncing off a rock which
naturally we called "Bounce Rock"
because it's our prerogative
like Adam to name things,
abrade surfaces, drill holes
in the rusty fabric of dead planets —
it's what we do

now solar-propelled *Curiosity*
geared to shovel pay-dirt —
signs of ancient water, methane,
maybe life, once, alluvial fans
and sand-ripples a map
of our own future

Bradbury's imagined world
dessicated, long gone,
eroded rock strata scattered
like the bones of Martians
on the edge of craters

cute, personable, robots
way beyond their use-by date
learn too late
what might be useful tomorrow

Everyday surveillance

we're fearful of drone-addicts spying
on our stripped-down me-time, backyard
pool antics, but Facebook's got us pinned
already – Big Data harvested
as we browse like snails unhinged
from their shells: unbidden, ads pop up
for soulmates, cat caboodles,
       seven types of home-made pasta

it's raining drones, and we go about
our ordinary terror, watched,
surveyed, secured from above.
because "something might happen",
we're wired to ICT, tethered
to IDs, tracked by the spoors we leave,
       caught in a Web of our own choosing

Fat Controllers
sit in air-conditioned comfort
clutching joysticks, 'cubicle warriors'
grafted onto Predators.
the skies, emptied of their usual
deities, are chock-a-block
with phantom limbs, lethal insects
       liquidating human targets

Dualities

wildfires and rogue winds and what bullets do to bodies   but we can
make ice in the desert   detect black holes colliding by the ripples in
space-time   gulp lime-green gelatine with our goldfish mouths   and
call it food   astronauts free-floating in weightlessness   somewhere
in the constellation *Scutum* Pioneer II ploughs on   ambassador for
humanity   out of touch with Earth   but bearing a plaque   an image
of a man and a woman   a spacecraft   a map of the galaxy and our
location in it   just so *they* know where we live and what we know
foundations are shaking   new fissures zig-zag over surfaces   but we
cheerfully hazard-avoid among the stars   our names can be tweeted to
Mars better still our remains blasted into deep space   an everlasting
celestial journey   a star among stars ('environmentally benign,
surprisingly affordable') or as someone said 'kiss my ashes'

Un-earthed

Stepping in

theatre-bowl of a dry dam: we 'step in',
imagine, behind a curtain of dust
the soft seep of hidden springs
rivulets of run-off sliding across grass

frog-chatter   tick-tocking time-bombs
their silence alerts us to the advent
of a drier regime – whitened sheep skulls in gullies,
shards of earth the colour of failed barley

it's as though we're inside a crazed teapot,
standing at the bottom of a dry dam
mud turning itself inside out in a last grimace.
the Spectroradiometer on NASA's *Terra* satellite

gathers vegetation greenness data: the brown arc
of this place   below-average   attests to a drying trend
yabbies burrowing into some other century
sunken memories of tree-trunks and reeds

cracks and fissures in the wide brown land
after a long dry spell   we can scarcely remember
the earth alive with tiny frogs   or farmers, hats held out
to a frown of sky   dancing in brief transitory rains

Not all "sweetness and light"

diving into yourself
dredges mysteries and menace
trains on fire   birds in flight
snakes coiling from the hands
of faintly threatening women
some prefer the therapy of brush
and scumbled paint   working it out
as they go along   or you can wipe
the paint off altogether
                              start again
try to nail it before you lose it,
the same with words
(not that there's an answer
only that there's stillness   sometimes)

a sense of foreboding lies coiled
in uneasy terrain — these flanks of hills
furrowed and trenched, shadowy.
omen bird pendent in a black sky
flies to God or devil   no moon tonight,
just that eerie half-lit blue
like news from somewhere
bright boomerang of bird mandala
you night-flier above bruised slopes
                              falling
into serrated darkness   planetary death
        or the beautiful abyss
marked yours   and mine

Tribes killing tribes

Truth is ugly. We possess art lest we perish of the truth.
— Schopenhauer

Pisgah mountains bare fangs   not promises
the bird has not fought its way out of the egg
moonlight hills flow like a sea divided
cosmic observers eye the way
         we've made a hash of it
refugees or pilgrims herded or harvested
the Peruvian bat flies in on cue
with its lance of green   not so evil maybe
         only threatened

reality's a rock-face that offers few holds
Atlas Mountains or Indian hills
are flickering signifiers   enigmatic
         fractured
this is earth as we've made it   eroded gullies
wormholes snaking down hillsides
         gridlock of bare bones
with the world-ore gouged out
no Red Sea but a black canal
         reflecting cool blue light

Bird in search of a cage

eyes on stalks lean closer
watchers snaking across the sky
the bird is somewhere out of sight
                flying towards the cage
a red-in-tooth-and-claw cat
                stretches on the floor below
taut as a violin string
dreams of you in her jaws
the dog slowly licks the bars
        (friend or foe, friend or foe?)

was Freud right
and the meaning of life is death?
beaks ready to tear you to pieces
ontological anxiety
safer to hole up inside
peer through wire
bird in the middle ground
        preening your feathers
head cocked for cosmic violence
the world is woven through with meanings
        you never get to choose

Tread lightly

my shoes crush the brittle crust of earth
those signs near the Delicate Arches:
do not disturb the membrane
these plants depend on for survival

red earth of Utah speaks to me
in that knobbly crunch of algae
and lichen   pinnacles or pedicles
I trample unwittingly   sheathes
of cyanobacteria buried where no light
will reach them: death under every footfall

my cells recall syllables of smoke unseen
each leaf and twisted trunk   each shape
and shade of the old people   half-animal
half-human   spiralling through my dreams

Earthed

Finding Mangrove Mountain

ten years old, you're curled up on the back seat
sick from petrol fumes. beyond the window
grey-green whorls of gum-trees
scrub clutching at sandstone, trunks dangling
their tapestry of bark. flamingo-legs spindle
above, winged branches woven with sky.
on the road ahead, double yellow lines ribbon
and unspool, sun-struck sandstone makes shadows
streak and shine in rivulets down gullies.
the Vanguard bursts from tree-tunnels
into sun-haze, light splashing silver round every bend.

Charlie's ramshackle farm signals
from another dimension, past fallen fences,
hidden driveways, letter-boxes telegraphing
Dun-Torken and *Thistledome* —"What does
that mean, Dad?" (he's too busy telling
Gary how to work the clutch)

you work your way back to a grove of trees,
splinters of memory, Charlie's lean-to shed
half-choked with rambling roses, purple bougainvillea
spilling over saplings tied with twine. only fragments
remain: Copper the draught-horse looms in the barn,
hens scatter in the long grass. a fleeting cameo
of you running your own mad race
through citrus orchard fingerlings of light

this is the sum of memory: impressions
of a half-wild place on the edge of bush.
tree-trunks were castle walls stretched tall,
and you spiralled up through leaves

and thorns to stained-glass windows winking
yellow light. the din of cicadas filled the day,
the road ahead a dark snake uncoiling
across the mountain. the world was bigger
than you knew — you could breathe there,
trees gave you air, dark shadows swooped.
that was the beginning.

Two views

1. mangrove country

a bird's-eye view opens out, raptor-eye drilling
down to dreaming tracks, acupuncture
of oyster-leases and grey-blue mangroves
on the Hawkesbury. bodies surface
from time to time, mud-embalmed, sluiced
into daylight, but you feel coffined, boots sinking
in the mud. *Avicennia marina* crouch inwards,
thin snouts of pneumatophores poke
above the water, mini-periscopes spying nothing.
upriver   oysters, starved to death, ingest their own gonads

2. mangroves with oyster-beds
hike in strong boots to wherever a good <u>there</u> is
– Rachel du Plessis

a *Toccata and fugue* builds and swells in cathedrals
of green   stilt-roots lift gothic arches out of the mud
amphibious, like us, they keep a toe-hold between salt
and fresh water. germinating seed-pods spiral in eddies,
sow futures without end, mangrove flowers perfect
as roses, millions of stars floating loose on the current

you crouch on taut thighs shucking oysters, hair
alive with cinders. flames dervish in the fireplace,
a kind of healing. studs of moisture, molten on glass,
are self-contained as embryos, or pearls

Tuggerah Lake reverb

I take the track down from the house
through waist-high grass
where black snakes used to live
until my father sliced and diced them
with a sheet of corrugated iron, draped
their bloody coils on the front porch

like a trophy. across the water,
pencilled outlines of The Entrance
waver and retreat. somewhere
under all this, the detritus of years:
my brother's name, carved on rock
cinders of a bushfire that circled
as I crouched in the shallows,
my mother walking into the bush,
holding her head in her hands.

sedge-grasses eclipsed me,
a small girl wandering,
swinging shade of she-oaks
falls away
to renovated shacks, cabanas
and chlorine pools clamped tight
on marshland and scrub.

reflection offers a softer edge,
a fuller sound in this open space;
I wade along that shore, pick my way
across clumps of stack-weed
heaped like mangled brains.
the long wild grass is gone,
a tamed Reserve the local dogs
are duty-bound to guard

memory's gated reverb
punches out percussion, moments
amplified, disrupted sound waves.
time decides how long they take
to decay, what repercussions curl
onto a shore I visit and revisit,
mostly in dreams. nothing
and everything is as it was.

Fire hawks accused of arson

arsonists firebrand slow-burning grasslands
we want it to be true
because there's knowing
and there's really knowing:
watching you swoop in low
a burning twig gripped
in black talons   tongues of flame
licking the highway
where you glide and rise
          as grass catches fire

black kites spreading fire to flush out
prey   another order of knowing
Waipuldanya's eye-witness account
of our "little troublemaker"
dismissed as legend –
now scientists are all fired up
to grant intentionality
to avian smarts (guessing
where there's smoke there's fire)

dark shadows wheel in burnt-orange light
sharp-eyed opportunists scoop up
smouldering snakes   char-grilled mice
and some of us are more than willing
          to concede the incendiary ways of birds

Builders and shakers

Trees and stones will teach you that which you can
never learn from masters. – Saint Bernard de Clairvaux

under a fierce sun some termite mounds
are gnarled shark-fins erupting from the sand
tower-builders   soldiers powered by one mind
super-bug architects don't need hard hats
to fabricate their ideal space
technology's embedded in their DNA

Harvard scientists probe the collective mind
engineers drill into dirt mounds   peer
into chambers   bio-mimic insect swarms
with pygmy robots – autonomous
unsupervised   without a plan – rebuilding
in post-disaster zones   or on Mars

in the savannah of Namib simple rules
apply   repair the mound   farm fungi
keep the nest stable   spread the word
through touch and vibration   pile chamber
upon chamber   purposeful   driven
mound over mound   like some ancient tribe
building for the life to come
your termite queen's no queen
of the desert   legless   fat   palpitating
she's a captive ovary churning out millions
her entire life   for the rest   it's plugging gaps
mouths full of dirt   racing against rain

Eel odyssey

1.
see her wide-mouthed grin rising
from the murk   siren-singing
soon-to-be sojourner on the seas
top predator in the pond at home
her feral-spotted scales
silvered in moonlight

flirty-finned and lithe
as Esther Williams in the pool
not so *dangerous when wet*
she's a 20-million-egg mermaid
mooching after ducklings
crunching young carp
with plate-like teeth

but change is coming   a ripening:
at autumn's rainy imperative
she'll up stakes   undulate
from park or edgy dam
swimcrawlslide from fresh
to brackish to salt   slither
through wetland and golf-course
by night   fin-over-fin
through corridors of swamp
and sedge-grass   down
past the third runway
to pour the dark wine
of her body into Botany Bay

2.
up there in the Coral Sea
she's a voyager horizontal-nosing
in the depths by day   vertical
as an exclamation mark
by night   gut and anus

dissolved – no more eating
her body's silver now
lured by moon and tides
or some Pangaean memory
to spawn in warmer waters
where she began
exhausted   she'll die there
in new-moon days
drift to the bottom of a deep dark sea

Feather star

clenched fist   night-fingers reaching
from the underworld   a feather star creeps
from rock crevice to coral outcrop
ribbons of green and yellow
rising and falling in darkness

like coral unfettered   undulating fronds
are sticky catch-alls funnelling food
pursued   the crinoid soft-pedals away
sinks to the sea-floor   tarantula crouching
in torchlight   no brain   no eyes
but evolved to outlast the dinosaurs

free-swimming from sea-star or grasping crab
strolling mouth in a carnival-mask
it twirls in the current like a dancer
drifter in a world of drifters

Head-banger

try being a woodpecker for a change – head-banging
on his favourite tree 12,000 times a day,
knocking like a builder under eaves, quizzical
head poised, tongue breaking into song.
drumming on a dying tree, he goads the hunter
with his gun, who says the bones are only good for soup

he can show you true hard-headedness, what it is
to use your head like a battering ram, without
the headache. we can learn from him,
channel some of that "nature-inspiration".
admit it – he's got a good head on his shoulders.
no bird-brain, his keen eyes and natural rhythm
come in handy for rustling up a meal,
or drumming up a mate

once it was drummed into our heads that the news
from the universe wasn't worth knowing, nothing more
than primitive mumbo-jumbo, and that our apex position in –
forgive me – the pecking order was assured
but some bright spark's already borrowed
the woodpecker's *modus operandi* –
voilà, we have the uber-hard cardboard helmet,
spin-off from his tau-charged brain,
super-light head-bones and flexible cartilage.
(three times stronger than polystyrene)
as for the woodpecker, success
hasn't gone to his head – yet –
it sure beats having it brought in on a platter

Ridge-walking

for all you know these ridges
are as old as the halos that traverse
Saturn's moon   or light-swept canyons
on Mars   creeping black sand dunes
fractured with rocky outcrops

up here time drops out of sight
a passing eagle   the bush folds out
into space   you feel it   this crest
pushes you like a wave   further and further
along its sloping surface   and you're no longer

breathless   the climb's behind you
(town nowhere to be seen)
no longer just putting one foot
in front of the other but embedded
among the scribble of leaves
smear of branches   patchwork of trees

stretching away to the horizon
you can see your way clear now
launched into that hazy beyond
the smell of smoke and leaf-mulch
spiralling through the air

Pruning dogwood in late autumn

cracking dry branches with bare hands,
I toss them in the bin —
either this dogwood's past its use-by date
or I'm unseasonal, pruning late, pruning early

this one-time execution-tree —
broken daggers, lop-sided
ready to pack it in —
just so much dead wood
hardly load-bearing enough
for a full-on crucifixion
or sacrificial love

leaves quiver, cling to sunlight
Chaucer's whippletree
pokes out its tongues of flame,
      tastes lightness
hangs out for another shot at summer

Saving the Pines, January 2020

your closest relatives are Hoop and Bunya,
Norfolk, Kauri and Monkey Puzzle.
more of a puzzle how you survived,
weathered the rifting of continents,
the passing of the age of reptiles.
male and female together
in the one tree, dangling male cones
drifting pollen to female cones above,
spiked sputniks of seed unpalatable
to marauding mouths

one of the best-kept secrets in the world,
pathogen-shy Wollemi can be felled
by microscopic life on human boots.
every one of your adult and juvenile trees
shares the exact same DNA.
it was a mega-fire that almost did you in,
the Gospers Mountain wall of flames,
a new phase of what some are calling
the sixth great extinction. all around you
the browned-off silent forest
a more ordinary devastation –
no redemption there

air-dropped in, yellow-jacketed saviours
doused you in water, cascading
fire-retardant on woodland ahead
of the flames. huddled in gorges
against Triassic sandstone cliffs,
you were 'forest-bathing' with a difference.
two on your flank were scorched and scarified
but you survived, as you have snow-storms
and lightning strikes and the towering jaws of sauropods.

you roamed the world, once, giant conifers
of Laurasia and Gondwana, then disappeared
shrank back to this precious motherlode,
fires extinguished for now in a daring
human intervention, protected by the seed
of mammals that on warm wet tropical nights
once scurried at your feet

In the moment

back to a late afternoon sky   a wedge of escarpment still bright
with a flush of sunlight on sandstone trapped at day's end
a map of stone ill-defined above a neighbour's photinia
(filtered glimpses of views that haven't budged
since Darwin found us wanting)

morning mist makes gothic mouths above the pebbled drive
swelling and muscling through branches like Michelin Man
at this ungodly hour   headlights punching darkness

threading ourselves onto a string of tail-light beads
we fall into place   speedy   impatient   half-awake
an hour or more of Russian roulette with predatory trucks
survival of the fittest our daily interactive game

in the rear-vision mirror   a solitary gumtree
ghostly in moonlight
bare trees armed with the promise of buds

Not hearing the world

it's insidious, the slow creep of moss
that stifles sound, hair cells blunted
in the ear, the world drowned out

sometimes you opt for silence
over amplification, the rattle and clack
of unfiltered noise — there's no effort

in denial; you take the line of least resistance
when sound knocks itself out, indecipherable
codes buzzing in antechambers of bone

friends become mutterers, untrustworthy oracles:
backs turned, on the wrong side of you,
they're fogged-up windows, closed bank doors

inland, past the auricles, a tide of sound
sweeps into the canal, only the eardrum's
less up-beat these days, much less flows

the organ of Corti grown dull, ossicles
fused with bone, the body's microphone
switched off. along the nerve cells

it's a domino effect, sensorineural breakdown,
auditory structures failing, falling,
shimeji mushrooms soggy and leaning

anyone's guess what's next — brain atrophy,
lost pathways ("you might lose hearing in both ears",
the specialist intones in cheerful prophecy). of course

there's grief – you think of your maternal grandmother
laying hands on the tv like a Pentecostal, feeling
the rhythm of music she would never hear

the shrill notes of songbirds grow fainter, fade,
wind wheezes, coal-trains threading through mountains
scrape like wind forced through the eye of a needle

now for you, too, consonants break away from words
their pitch lost on you,
ice floes calving into a frozen sea

Waking at night

no horror now, awake at night, no intruder flowing
from window to unlocked door, a child huddled
in a tangle of blankets on the floor
                              impaled with fright

no thoughts of forced entry, a torch-beam's white light
oozing under the door   noises in the night
are only possums hip-hopping
on corrugated iron, breaking it down
                              in a Cupid Shuffle

a streetlight glows through blinds, the moon's
rimmed with mist, but dimness is just dimness
                              unpopulated, benign

liquid notes dissolve into words on a page, rain
and Rachmaninov keep time
                              on hold, for now

Hearing the world

mid-mountain, you feel the weather coming in,
palpable, drifts of fog and nimbostratus
infiltrating from the Southern Highlands.
past the village sign you know you're home,
behind you now the four-car prang,
blue flashing lights, the glitter and crunch
of debris on the road, the rubber-necking
at what has kept you idling for an hour.
tonight, you're unscathed. clouds
are gravid with tomorrow's snow

all the forecasts agree
an extreme weather event
is on the cards, though the Bureau
insists on calling it a 'cold front'
not 'Antarctic vortex'.
pity – you like the drama
and magnitude of it, global weirding
with a vengeance. it still takes you
by surprise next morning, like in Oxford
all those years ago, your first sight of snow,
fat postcard-robins on silvery
branches, hyperreal, the whole world
transformed, and you, in that moment.

step into the garden on a slide
of ice, the dog-bowl topped
with a furry pane of glass,
a tarpaulin of snow stretched tight across
the crinkle-cut roof of the old garage.
padding across the yard, Frieda
leaves dark lacunae in her wake,

spoor disappearing into white-out.
you wonder if the Falls below
are suspended in ice,
like a Hokusai wave about to break

suddenly, driving becomes
a dangerous idea, why risk it
for your workaday routine,
coming down from the mountain to the
flat plains of what you do for a living?

Live Traffic Reports whistle you
off the journey, and you make
the necessary call. workaholic,
you will never leave off feeling guilty
for the windfall of a day at home.

the cat, incarcerated indoors,
peers behind a Roman blind
at ghost-white trees, an unfamiliar
stretch of lawn. the flight of birds
is stilled, their startled childlike cry,
the Buddha fountain silent among
the ivy. short curls crusted with snow
mean renunciation, but half-closed eyes
look inward and outward, long earlobes
hear what's needed in the world

Covid cocktail

it's a day for purging, standing
on a stepladder throwing old sheets
over her shoulder like salt
for good luck. smart thinking,
offloading her surplus
to charity bins, death-cleaning
in a crisis, knowing she's shaken
by a micron smaller
than a human hair

time on her hands, or is it end-time,
muddled by enforced inertia
anxiety seeping in
some call it 'working from home'
she's glad to be doing something
while not mixing, so she pours
the Chambord down the sink,
the whole fat-bellied bottle,
every last drop

watches it swirl, the colour of blood,
black raspberries infused
with Madagascan vanilla
blackcurrant and cognac.
order. something predictable.

now she reads that Chambord
is meant for cocktails,
a base ingredient
for a Grateful Dead
or Purple Hooter Shooter –
has she squandered
yet another opportunity?

outside, pale morning.
everything's moving, waving,
straining at the leash. the elements
of her day are layered, floating
on top of one another:
pound the keyboard, plant bok choy,
pour Sambucca over ice.
whatever it takes. a twist of lime
a shot in the dark
out of these she builds her day

Breathing: shadows, trees, cloud

For Maocat

It is still beautiful to feel your heart throbbing
 But often the shadow feels more real than the body.
— Tomas Transtromer, *After Someone's Death*

just yesterday she'd stretched out on the grass, choosing sunlight,
rehearsal for the end, chin on paw, slowly seeping. flies came,
as they must — she had no energy to twitch them away.
I mounted guard while she dozed, her sides gently rising
and falling, I the servant to her dying queen, waving grass stems
like peacock feathers at flies on tail, chin, paw.
three times I left her alone, asking death to make it easy
for me, only to find her at dusk, breathing so slowly,
long drawn-out breaths, shivering dandelion heads

at the end she did not want to be alone with death coming.
I would want that too, gentleness, to be held — so much worse
to have no one, with darkness folding moth-wings overhead.
no voice we recognise, son, friend, family. the gloved hands
of strangers. she spoke surrender to what is coming.
I was *her* familiar, my disguise human, a gauze-dimmed shape
in the darkness shadowing her eyes, signalling release

we hesitated, standing over the grave, our own breathing suspended.
shadows passing over black fur — clouds scudding, trees leaning above —
was that a breath? I could not throw the first clod. could not play god.
those past weeks watching, waiting to see the fur move, lift, subside,
small messages to the world. but today she did not unfurl, did not shake
the dirt from her small face. we stood there, watching her final shape
nested in earth, cat-curled as though alive, tail encircling her, the last word

A tea-rose for Frieda, *Deutsche Shäferhund*

I peel layers: white gift-bag   kitsch brown box patterned
like Christmas and tied with a brown ribbon   and inside
a vacuum-sealed bag with the cloud-grey dust
                    of your too-brief life

fur-tufts still blow across the gravel path   the green rubber ball
rests near the fountain like a good intention   your shade
patrols the fence-line to spook the neighbour's chickens

in your last weeks I'd step into the night with torch-glare
stare down stars that dwarfed me – your eyes flickering
on and off like glow-worms – haul you back again
from darkness to a warm soft bed

Ferlinghetti says   dogs are realists
wiser than me   you were trying to let go
hung back when I reached for you
drifting into shadow   a ghost already
melting away to your favourite plot
under the lilac tree   that spot
where you'd lie, alive, among fallen leaves
turning the clivea to mush with your big body
your big invaded body

but here are candles and a perfect pink camellia
in a bowl   the neighbour's gift   a bi-coloured tea-rose
for your black-and-tan   *Baronne Edmonde von Rothschilde*
hunkers down for winter in the garden bed you dug up
in your frenzy   hunting forgotten bones   scattering the path
          with soil and mulch

all in all   your demands were small but insistent   you'd have ruled
the roost if I'd let you   I cursed you often   but find it fitting
that you're scattered here   in the promise of a wildly perfumed rose
your passion come full circle

Acknowledgments

The Best Australian Poems 2010 (Black Inc.), *Antipodes:* poetic responses, ed. Margaret Bradstock (Phoenix Publications, 2011), *Guide to Sydney Rivers*, ed. Susan Adams & Les Wicks (2015), *Diverse Poets* (2014), *Caring for Country*, ed. Margaret Bradstock (Phoenix Publications, 2017), *Contemporary Australian Poetry*, ed. Martin Langford, Judith Beveridge & David Musgrave (Puncher & Wattmann, 2017), *Live Encounters*, ed. Susan Hawthorne (2018), *Grieve* (Hunter Writers Centre, 2018), *Arrival* (*Lost in Books*, 2018), *Wild Voices*, ed. David Bassett (2019), *foame* (March 1, 2020), *Messages from the Embers:* From Devastation to Hope, An Australian Bushfire Anthology, ed. Julia Kaylock and Denise O'Hagan (2020), and *Burrow* Issue 1, September 1, 2020, ed. Phillip and Jillian Hall.

"Hearing the World" was Highly Commended in the 2018 Bruce Dawe Poetry Competition. A revised version was re-published in *Mountain Secrets* ed. Joan Fenney (Ginninderra Press, 2019).

'Stepping in' found its inspiration from John R. Walker's painting *The Dry Dam, Bedervale*, 2004.